THE
Archive Photographs
SERIES

WOODHOUSE
THE SECOND SELECTION

Twelve members of the Handsworth Sword Dancers at the Market Cross in 1975.

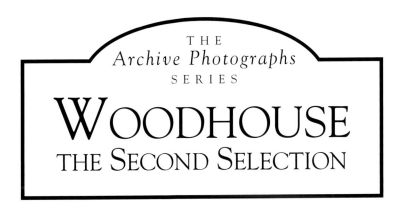

THE
Archive Photographs
SERIES

WOODHOUSE
THE SECOND SELECTION

Leonard Widdowson

TEMPUS

A group of Britannic Assurance officials with their wives and families, *c.* 1912. They pose in the front garden of the company's branch office at No. 51 Station Road, Woodhouse. This photograph appears on the book cover.

First published 1998, reprinted 2005

Tempus Publishing Limited
The Mill, Brimscombe Port,
Stroud, Gloucestershire, GL5 2QG
www.tempus-publishing.com

British Library Cataloguing in Publication Data.
A catalogue record for this book is available from the British Library.

ISBN 0 7524 1088 1

Typesetting and origination by Tempus Publishing Limited.
Printed in Great Britain.

Contents

Introduction   7

Acknowledgemets   8

1. The Village Centre   9

2. Cross Street, Chapel Street and Tannery Street   23

3. Market Street and Beaver Hill Road   41

4. Station Road and Woodhouse Mill   51

5. Shirtcliffe Wood and Vicar Lane   63

6. Beighton Road to Cliff Wheel   71

7. Sally Clarks and Birley East Pit   77

8. Birley Spa   85

9. The West End and Normanton Springs   97

10. Woodhouse People   113

A 1933 aerial view reminds us of much of pre-war Woodhouse.

Introduction

What changes happened in Woodhouse in the late 1960s! The village centre was transformed and buildings were swept away, among them the much loved Picture Palace, a centre point of the village. New shops, with first floor living accommodation, were erected and Market Place was pedestrianised. A new road was constructed from Tannery Street, which ran behind The Cross Daggers and The Stag public houses to join Market Street. This caused the loss of old lanes such as Malthouse Lane, Hoyland Lane, Orchard Terrace and Back Lane - although there still is a No. 1 Back Lane! Skelton Lane takes its name from the family of Skeltons, who owned the land where the library is built, which is now a busy road. Tannery Close, off Tannery Street, joins up with the Skelton Lane roads to make a large housing estate, on the south side of Tannery Street. Land that was once occupied by houses and shops (including the post office), from the beginning of Sheffield Road up to the by gone Pashleys Cottages, is now land occupied by Tannery Lodge. How many remember Cockayne's Yard which was also there?

Across the road, on the odd numbered side up to No. 19 Sheffield Road, are the two and three storey flats on Skelton Grove, land where Waterslacks Lane and Sheffield Road houses once stood. Brick Row, The Pawnshop, Garden Walk and the Allotment Gardens are all just memories now. Not all of the new housing developments were built on land vacated as a result of property being demolished. A glance at the 1933 aerial view (see p. 6) shows open land beyond St James church where, in the 1950s, the Tithe Barn Estate was built. At the top of the view we can see parts of fields which now contain the Badger Estate. Also on this picture, Revill Lane can be clearly seen before it passes the clump of trees of the old cemetery. It joins Beaver Hill Road and Hawksworth Croft is to its right. The top corner (right) shows the recreation ground with Pringle Field on its left. Apart from the remaining houses on the right of Sheffield Road and the library and the Vestry building, the whole of the bottom right quarter has changed. Going further west, Victoria Road has been replaced with Swallow Wood Court, a name taken from the nearby coal seam, and Ashpool Close, a name chosen because of the Ash trees from which Ashwell Road gets its name. Old maps show that there was once a pond at the bottom of Victoria Road.

The changes did not stop there. Normanton Springs lost its rows of houses on Coisley Hill but gained much, when property was built around Haxby Street. At the other end of the village we have seen new property built off Beighton Road to rehouse the residents of the John Calvert and Greengate Roads area. Off Furnace Lane is Kirkstead Gardens, the name is taken from Kirkstead in Lincolnshire. In the thirteenth century monks from Kirkstead Abbey arrived there after being granted rights to use part of the mill for the purpose of grinding their corn. John Hibbard Avenue and Crescent are two new roads off Soaphouse Lane. John Hibbard was the owner of the nineteenth century Soap Works. These new homes in Woodhouse Mill help to restore the balance of property lost in previous years.

Birley Spa is over on the other side of Shirebrook and is not within the Woodhouse boundary. However, it has always been shared with the Hackenthorpe community and holds memories for older local people. Especially those who can recall the days before the Second World War, when boats were on the pond and all kinds of amusements were enjoyed. Now the grounds, pond and Bath House, with its Roman Bath, are all maintained by the dedicated volunteers of the Shirebrook Conservation Group, assisted by the Sheffield Countryside Management Unit. Every year since 1992, there has been an open day, organised by the Conservation Group as part of the events of the Annual Sheffield Environment Week, in the month of May. It is hoped that this will continue.

This second edition of over 200 different photographs and illustrations will help to fill in any gaps which, through lack of space, were left in the 1996 publication. It will show what, in many instances, has been lost as a result of demolition. The earlier photographs show village life in the days of big open fires, pegged rugs, tin baths on the hearth, gas mantles and Donkey stone. The days of the copper for boiling the washing, the Yorkshire ranges and the chore of black leading, but also the smell of home baked bread. In those days everybody had a Coop number and the school bobby visited truant's homes. The pictures evoke memories of the echoing sound of miners clogs and the voice and the bell of the oatcake and pikelet man. You did not bother to lock the door if you went to the corner shop or popped in to see a neighbour. Life went on at a more leisurely pace, as is evident from the old pictures. Finally, I hope this book gives as much pleasure to you as it has to me while compiling it.

L. Widdowson, 1998.

Acknowledgements

I thank all those who have helped me in producing this book, especially Marjorie Williamson who so willingly offered to type (from my handwriting) the information which accompanies the pictures. My thanks go to Alan Rowles for his excellent knowledge of Birley East Pit and for supplying the names of those men on the steam locomotives. Thanks also go to John Shepherd and Frank Coupe, always there to help in various ways, and Stanley Fox, Maurice La Dell, Coleen Rawlins, Ada Herbert, Joyce Jowle and Lily Machin. Also to my late father Stanley Widdowson who told me so much. He was born and bred in the village and would have enjoyed seeing the pictures of places he knew so very well. Other information, from before living memory, was gleaned from the books: *Woodhouse* by Ernest Atkins and *Le Talls Woodhouse* by Wm James Le Tall. We also owe our gratitude to those old photographers, who trudged around with their tripods and heavy cameras, for providing us with such a rich pictoral history.

One

The Village Centre

Sam Gillott stands in the doorway of his butcher shop in Market Place in the 1950s. Miss Mary Redfearn kept the Cross Daggers public house during the 1940s and '50s.

The Market Cross with two listed buildings behind it, the Cross Daggers and the adjacent shop, c. 1910. On the extreme left is the Meadow grocery shop, which later moved into larger premises in Market Street, shown as BuyWise on page 42, which now houses the Lotus House restaurant. Note the new top step of the Cross and the new pillar, which replaced an earlier one in 1897.

A pre-1897 look at the Market Cross showing the old pillar which was erected in 1775. When completed, the following names were inscribed upon it: Robert Johnson, John Newbold and Gilbert Inkersall. These three had the responsibility for arranging for the Cross to be erected at the time and yet it appears to have been paid for out of public funds. The date 1826, on the present pillar, is the year of the addition to it of the sundial and weather vane. The other date, 1897, is the year in which the old pillar was replaced with the new one and some renovation work carried out.

A wintry scene in Market Place in the 1950s. The Wizard shop, attached to the Cross Daggers on the corner of Malthouse Lane, along with the buildings in the background, are now just memories.

The Salvation Army Band marches through Market Place on a wet Sunday morning in January 1954.

The old Royal Hotel on the corner of Market Place and Tannery Street. It was demolished and replaced by the present Royal in 1938. The two stone stoops of the stocks have yet to have their wooden beams put back. In Tannery Street we can see Keyworth's butcher shop, later to become Henry Wheeler's Gents Hairdressers. The small building was the greengrocery shop of Mr J. Hill during the 1930s.

J. Hill advertisement as it appeared in the Woodhouse church magazine of 1931, along with three other well known shops.

The buildings to the right of the Royal Hotel were subsequently demolished to make way for a new row of shops.

A bird's eye view of Market Square. Prominent in the centre is the Picture Palace with Hardcastles Yard to its right.

The Woodhouse Picture Palace and two small shops, occupied by Don Valley (Cleaners) Ltd and Mr Fox's drapery shop, are shown in this 1950s photograph. The building in brick and embossed concrete was constructed on a site in 1914 where there had previously been shops. The contractor was John Longdon and Sons. The cinema opened on 2 March 1914 with the silent film *Kissing Cup*. Forty three years later, on Saturday 28 December 1957, the cinema closed. The last film shown was *Twelve Angry Men*.

Market Place with the row of four shops known locally as Dickinson's Corner. Before the Second World War this was the 3 Q w d fare stage, by bus, from Sheffield. For an extra Q w d you could extend your journey to the terminus at the railway station.

Hobbies, copies of this one penny, weekly magazine cover the whole window of Dickinson's first shop.

Coo Hill, behind the War Memorial. 'Coo hill in the centre of the village has had the north boundary raised by a retaining wall and the surface levelled by the Urban District Council. Iron railings have been placed there as a protection to the public.' (Wm James Le Tall, October 1899.) An earlier comment from the same source, 'Coo Hill at that time had much Wormwood and Buckbean growing in it.'

Coo Hill and Church Lane. The building at the bottom of the hill was originally a Malt House. 'There, I have often watched workmen turning over the barley with very large wooden shovels.' (Ernest Atkin, 1950.) Later it became the Central Hall and showed silent films. After the First World War it became the Oasis Refreshment and Billiard Hall.

Coo Hill and Market Street. Mason's sweet shop is on the corner of Market Street and Orchard Terrace.

An earlier view of the beginning of Market Street shows the now demolished buildings on the right, where the Job Centre and car park now stand.

A group of people gathered to see the Woodhouse Wagon on its first day in 1975.

A neat row of modern shops now stand in the precinct where the slope of Coo Hill was.

That part of the precinct shortly afterwards, with all the new shops now occupied.

R & D Smeldey's shoes and fancy leather goods shop. The shop, barn and house were all part of Hawksworth's property. The premises stand at the entrance to the field where the Woodhouse Feast assembled every year in the third week in August.

Yvette Fashions occupied the premises before the building was renovated.

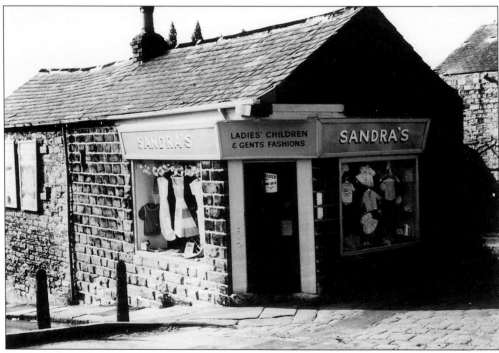

Sandra followed Yvette. Then, in 1987, J. White became the proprietor, she called the shop Eyecatchers. Next came Kath's Boutique and then Julies Too. Julie has long since gone and at the present time No. 33a Market Street remains empty. Since George Hawksworths days as a butcher, Kendalls and Barnards are among the many who have rented this shop.

Church Lane. The second pair of cottages on the left were demolished c. 1970. Just beyond is the space where the village Blacksmith's used to stand, set back off Church Lane.

The board on the side wall reads, W. Walker Shoeing and General Smith.

Down Malthouse Lane to Market Place. The two stone stoops on the left stand at the entrance to the Zion chapel.

Malthouse Lane crosses Back Lane and ends with the last house of the row, which can be seen in the background.

Two
Cross Street, Chapel Street and Tannery Street

The nearest building on the left existed before living memory, in Cross Street.

Cross Street from the bottom of Malthouse Lane. Note how narrow the road was outside the Royal Hotel in the 1950s. Having previously been a Thomas Rawsons public house and here advertising Gilmours Windsor Ales, it was finally taken over by Joshua Tetley of Leeds.

Cross Street, *c.* 1960. The buildings, where the white van is parked, were later demolished.

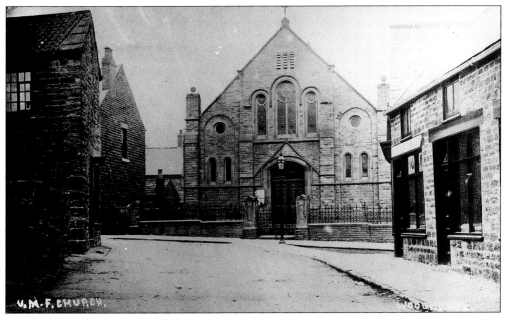

The UMF church or St Pauls Methodist church, as it was known, was erected on a site donated by George Widdison. The cost of the building was £1,477 and the first service was held on 1 October 1890. The minister was the Reverand H.T. Chapman of Leeds.

No. 10 and No. 12 Cross Street just before they were demolished in November 1983.

Manor Farm Cottage in a dilapidated condition. The lintel stone over the door has the letters EW and the year 1690 inscribed upon it. Past tenants here have included Richard Bartholemew (farmer), after whom the nearby Bartholemew Court was named. Other occupants were Charles W. Siddall and Thomas Whitaker, a partner in the mineral water business of Fowler, Whitaker and Cheetham. The last occupants were Mrs Alice Carthy and her two daughters, before the cottage was renovated.

Manor farm Cottage in 1982, shortly after its restoration.

Cross Street at its junction with Chapel Street. A Whitsuntide parade is seen from the frontage of St Pauls church in the 1920s.

The Woodhouse Wesley Church Band in Chapel Street. This image was caught moments before the one above.

Woodcocks advertise as Paperhangers, Signwriters and Decorators in Chapel Street. Thomas Woodcock, painter and decorator is listed in the 1902 directory.

The side of part of the old Angel Inn, in Chapel Street, in 1924.

The three ladies are walking past the front of the part of the old Angel Inn shown in the last picture. The sign board on the wall has the name Harry Pashley on it. He kept the Angel Inn from 1912 until 1925 and married Eva Mallinder the daughter of Horatio and Fanny Mallinder, who were the licencees before him. Early nineteenth-century records show both Thomas and Mary Widdison running the business and the inn was then called The Bull. There are many instances in Woodhouse where the wife carried on the business after her husband died. James Littlewood occupied the premises from 1851 until 1863 and it was during this time that the name was changed to the Angel Inn. William and Elizabeth Staniforth followed James Littlewood and were there until the Mallinders took over, *c.* 1886. All this property was demolished in 1925, for road widening, and the license was transferred to the present building in Sheffield Road. Ernest Dyson, a butcher by trade and employed by the British and Argentine Meat Company, in Market Place, became the first landlord at the new Angel Inn.

The premises of Williamson Bros Motor Engineers are set back from the demolished property of the picture on page 29.

The two well known Woodhouse names, of Mr W.N. White MPS, the chemist and Mr J. Shepherd, general draper, on these shops have now changed. Otherwise the view in Chapel Street remains the same.

The old Bakehouse behind J. Shepherd's property, before restoration. Note the wooden hoist which remains as a feature in the new design.

The Bakehouse is seen here during its conversion into residential dwellings.

This was the approach drive to Newton Croft, when it was the residence and surgery of Doctor Jackson.

Newton Croft. The surgery door is on the left.

Bernard Coulson outside his home, c. 1930. These cottages occupied the land where the post office later stood (until 1994). The post office premises are now occupied by Dickinsons newsagents.

The cottages, shown in the top picture, stood in the gap where the first cars on the left are parked. The two houses were demolished shortly after this photograph was taken in 1970. Mr Richardson's greengrocery shop went to make way for the new Coop car park.

Woodhouse fruit and flower shop occupied the premises after Mr Richardson retired.

This old farm building, behind the shop, was demolished in 1988. It was one of the few buildings which served as a reminder of the many farms that once existed in Woodhouse.

No. 40 Tannery Street, before restoration. The nearest cottage used to be the registry office for births and deaths. The original two cottages have been converted into one dwelling.

A happy, mixed ages group ready for a few hours of voluntary work. Only the stone wall of the frontage to the old vestery offices has survived from the 1960s.

Harold Cook leads the Woodhouse Prize Band, in Tannery Street, in 1930. Note the scaffolding on the right, which was erected during the building of the Woodhouse library.

A 1960s winter in old Skelton Lane, showing the contrasting stone and brick built rows of houses, on the left, where modern three storey flats now stand. The row of four cottages were believed to have been occupied by nailmakers in the last century.

The Woodhouse Feast was held on land behind the library after losing its old site on Hawksworth Croft.

1082 Tannery Street, Woodhouse.

The buildings on the right of the road have been replaced by the new development of Tannery Close. The footpath on the left has been extended since the building of new Salvation Army premises in 1926.

Tannery Street farm is seen here, from two different angles, on the same day, c. 1965. The top picture shows the main entrance in Tannery Street. The other shows a rear view which, judging by the curtains and the intact roof, indicates that the farm was occupied. In contrast the small building on the extreme right is obviously empty. The front of this building can be seen on page 39. The old barn was used as Shepherds slaughterhouse in earlier times.

Mr Shepherd, standing in the doorway of his butchers shop. The shop next door was also owned by the Shepherds, the two were connected by a doorway through the inner wall.

Tannery House in Birks Avenue, *c.* 1900. Only a short time later houses were built on the near side of the Avenue.

On the right is a wall and the railings of the Old Tannery in Tannery Street. Behind it and underground there was a culvert which is shown in the picture below.

Part of the Tannery 'Head Goit' is believed to have been a watercourse from the pond which was opposite the Vestry Hall. On the date of inspection, 15 September 1971, it was recorded that access to it was gained from inspection covers outside the Salvation Army building and Tannery House. The height of the tunnel was 4 metres and its width 2 metres at this point. Recently, due to the collapse of part of the tunnel and subsidence, it has had to be filled in.

Three

Market Street and Beaverhill Road

G.L. Curr & Son and W. Slater Haigh MPS display prominent name boards over the windows of their shops in this photograph of Market Street, *c.* 1930.

In 1968 the occupants of the shops on page 41 became Roache & French and D.J. Tomlinson MPS. Evidence of some demolition can be seen in the background, where the 'chippy' stands today. (Photograph by courtesy of Sheffield City Library.)

Dales boot and shoe shop (later to become Hollis and Dale), in the same row as the shops above. Note the gas lighting in the window of this fine display of footwear.

From the bottom of Hoyland Lane we can see a much narrower Market Street with Burgins sweet shop on the left. Across the road is the first of the dozen or so houses known as Farmyard Cottages. The small wooden building, which was also part of the yard, was a fish and chip shop.

Eleven dwelling houses on the odd numbered side of Spa Lane, *c.* 1975. A steel wire band supports the bulging walls of stone cottages which were well over 100 years old. The cottages are shown on a Ground Plan of Buildings in Woodhouse in 1862. All of the cottages have now been demolished and the residents rehoused in newly built flats nearby.

The cobbled surface of Orchard Terrace from The Stag to Back Lane.

Back Lane at the top of Orchard Terrace. The building on the right (No. 1 Back Lane now) is the only one to remain of those seen in this 1960s photograph.

Hoyland Lane and the frontage of No. 1 Back Lane when the Dents lived there and ran their corner shop.

Looking down Hoyland Lane from the front of Dent's shop. On this sunny afternoon, in the 1960s, we can clearly see Tomlinson's chemists and Fugill's printers. The wide stone building had previously been a Salvation Army Hall and before 1889 was used by St Paul's Methodists. In 1889 they acquired a new chapel.

The back of the derelict shops in Market Street, as it was in 1985.

Revill Lane, c. 1963. The view has changed little in 35 years.

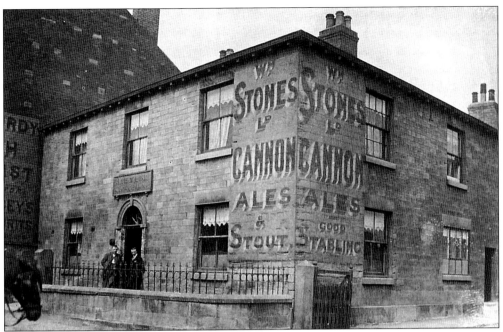

Albert Bird kept the George Inn for around 10 years, before the First World War. He is probably one of the two men standing in the doorway.

Compare this side view of The George, as it is now called, with the last picture. Another doorway has been added between the two downstairs windows. The wooden gate is obviously new, but the stone stoop looks remarkably similar to that in the previous picture.

On the corner of Market Street, opposite the top of Beaver Hill Road, is the building of W.J. Cooke & Sons, corn merchants. There is also a row of cottages with Meetinghouse Lane in the background.

Cooke's building and Carr House stand out prominently from the cleared site where Peartree Yard and the row of houses, seen above, once stood.

A front view of Cookes building with Maws House, coal dealers, on the left.

The footpath to the left of the trees was a part of Carr Lane, going up to join Market Street. In the background are the modern flats of Woodhouse Gardens, built on the land vacated when Peartree Yard and Cookes building were demolished.

Jabez Good captured this scene opposite the bottom of Hawksworth Croft, in Carr Lane. The word Carr describes common land, often marshy. It is a North Country and Midlands term. The land to the right, where the Badger Estate is now, slopes all the way to Woodhouse Mill, which had been known as Woodhouse Carr in the eighteenth century.

The houses in Goathland Road and Greenwood Lane can be seen behind the cyclists. We can also see a reminder of one of the two gas tanks which were situated in the village. Access to the tanks was gained from a lane opposite the Brunswick field in Station Road.

Four
Station Road and Woodhouse Mill

H. Jepson, bakers, on the corner of Station Road and Market Street. This is a scene reminiscent of old Woodhouse, with its assortment of buildings and chimney stacks.

Looking down Station Road from Jepson's shop in the 1960s. The glass ventilation structure of the Conservative Club can be seen behind the chimney pot on the left.

Woodhouse School in Station Road, built in 1889, had accommodation for 837 scholars. The headmaster, James Morton, and all the children were transferred from Endowed School. The new school became known as Morton's School because five of the Morton family taught there.

We can see here the corner shop on Tilford Road and Station Road, and the adjoining Oxfam shop, in 1982. The stone buildings are known as the Talbot Buildings. Before 1921, when Woodhouse became part of the City of Sheffield, Tilford Road, as it is now, was called Talbot Road.

The plaque over the door of the corner shop gives the date 1876 under the words 'Talbot Buildings'.

A tranquil scene with a horse drawn cart and its two occupants travelling up the middle of the road. The corner shop advertises Frys cocoa and Frys chocolate over the doorway.

These houses, off Station Road, were known as the Gas Houses. They were occupied by the families of men employed at the gas plant down the lane to the left (see page 50).

White lines, to mark the centre of the road, were once unnecessary, as we can see in this turn of the century photograph of another little changed scene. Edward's wooden shop (now gone) is in the background. A gas lamp stands at the top, where Goathland Road is now. Children stand and stare at the photographer, accompanied by just one adult, but the young girl is obviously very wary as she watches from behind the wall.

The Secondary School was built in 1909 by the West Riding Authority, it later became known as the Woodhouse Grammer School. It flourished until 1964 when it was absorbed into the new Aston Woodhouse High School at Swallownest.

The assembly hall of the Woodhouse Grammer School.

The well lit, spacious dining hall.

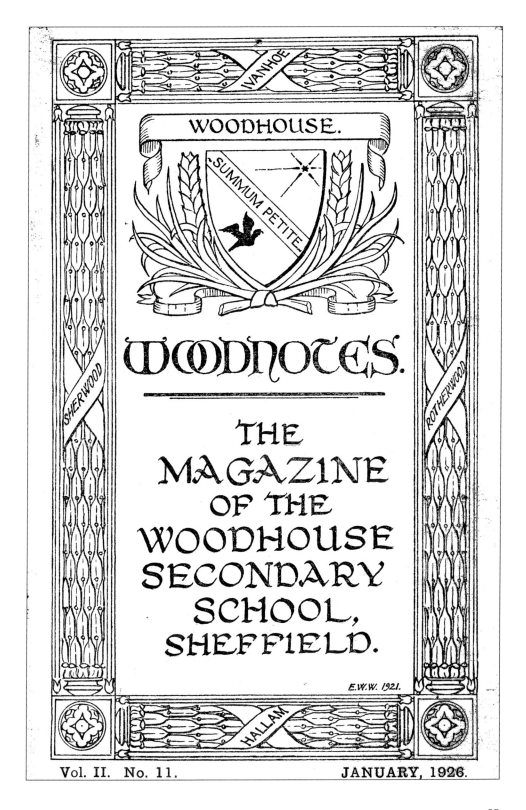

IVANHOE

WOODHOUSE.

SUMMUM PETITE

SHERWOOD

ROTHERWOOD

Woodnotes.

THE MAGAZINE OF THE WOODHOUSE SECONDARY SCHOOL, SHEFFIELD.

E.W.W. 1921.

HALLAM

Vol. II. No. 11.   JANUARY, 1926.

Furnace Lane takes its name from the furnace in Station Road, which was situated below where the old school stands now. A rental book shows an entry of 1s 6d paid, by John Marshall, for the furnace and land in 1755. The old cottages and the remains of the furnace were pulled down in 1899. Station Road was called Severside Lane and then Furnace Lane before the present name was adopted.

Looking along Worksop Road (now Retford Road) in the direction of Fence. On the extreme right we can see the old Princess Royal public house.

The Underwood Motor Bus is travelling towards Sheffield, here it is about to pass the bus stop outside the old Princess Royal, opposite Coalbrook Crescent. The present public house's address is No. 680 Retford Road and it has more frontage than its predecessor.

The primitive Methodist church building in Furnace Lane now serves the community as a DIY store.

Here we look down on Badger Sette Cafe and petrol pumps, a favourite refreshment stop for lorry and car drivers on the A57 road. The proprietors are Ernest and Mary Hall.

On the Island. Pictured, are Mrs Hobson (looking over the wall), Brenda Tomkins and Mrs Sarah Batham.

The Flood Control Regular and some of the houses seen, below and on page 58, where the Texaco filling station now stands.

Kingston Place, a *cul-de-sac* of around twelve houses.

The Woodhouse Mill War Memorial on its original site, on the corner of Furnace Lane and Retford Road. On Easter Monday 1922 the Bishop of Sheffield, Leonard Hedley Burrows, dedicated the memorial to the memory of the 39 men of Woodhouse Mill, Fence and Junction Road who lost their lives in the First World War. Those present with the Bishop included the Vicar of Woodhouse, Rev C.E. Hughes MA, Rev W.H. Brooke MA (Aston), Rev G.E. Johnson (Woodhouse), Mr G. Stokes (who officiated as Chairman) Councillor Ernest Atkin, Councillor T. O'Brien and Mr J.M. Thurston. As well as the many ex-servicemen present, the Woodhouse Prize Band was in attendance with The Buffs and the Boy's Life Brigade, under the command of Captain Horton. Nine more names have since been added to the memorial, those of men who died in the Second World War.

The remains of the old Roman road are still visible, during dry summers, in Treeton Dyke, Faulkner Lane. The road was part of the important Ryknield Street, which came from the Fosse Way near Cirencester, to Derby, Chesterfield and the Roman fort at Templeborough. From Chesterfield one route followed the course of the Tiver Rother. The other route came more directly to Templeborough by passing over Birley Moor to the west.

Five

Shirtcliffe Wood and Vicar Lane

A quiet moment, during prayers, at a Whitsuntide gathering on the Church Croft during the 1920s

Shirtcliffe House stood a few yards from Church Croft, in Church Lane. It was the home of Charles Hodgson, who was listed in an 1822 directory as a manufacturer of spades and shovels at the Woodhouse Mill Forge and Rolling Mills. He was a prominent Methodist and offered his house as accommodation for visiting preachers. Along with his brother George, he had a considerable influence on the movement during those early years.

A rare photograph of Caudle Well. This was a natural spring and was one of several places from which the village people would fetch their water in the last century. It was about 50 yards along the path into Shirtcliffe Wood, opposite the present South Yorkshire Fire and Rescue Service Brigades Training Centre, on Beaver Hill Road.

The entrance into Shirtcliffe Wood at the bottom of Beaver Hill Road. The wood was opened to the public by Bramley Firth in 1898.

The photographer's daughter poses on the bridge.

A couple pause on a bridge along the footpath through Shirtcliffe Wood to Handsworth.

The steps may have gone, but this is still the way out of the wood and over the fields to Handsworth.

These buildings were known as The Grange. This is where Beaver Avenue and Beaver Drive are situated now. The premises belonged to the firm of Fisher Son and Sibray, the nursery company.

A later picture of the same buildings, showing some of the modern houses on the Flockton Estate on the right. On the left is a small plot of land which was a place of interesting antiquity (see p. 68).

The overgrown, seventeenth-century private cemetery of the Stacye family of Ballifield Hall, c. 1950. Two of the eight gravestones are shown on page 69. Mahlon Stacye, a Quaker, emigrated to Trenton in New Jersey, USA, where he built a log dwelling in 1680. He was a Justice of the Peace and an active member of the Society of Friends. He died in 1704, but his descendants still live in the town of Trenton. The four roads off Beighton Road, Stacye Avenue, Stacye Rise, Trenton Close and Trenton Rise, were named after Mahlon Stacye's family and are permanent reminders of the final resting place of several of the Stacye family.

This unbroken stone reads 'Here Lyeth The Body Of Elizabeth Daughter Of Robert Stacye Of London Who Died The 11 of May 1667.

Another reads, 'Here Lyeth The Body Of Judith Wife Of Thomas Stacy Of Ballifield Who Died The 25 of November 1670'. A second person (most probably her husband) is mentioned on the stone, the date of death is given as 27 July 1683.

A group of children pose for this picture, which also shows up the cart wheel lines in the earthen surface of Vicar Lane.

The iron railings were removed to help the war effort. Otherwise, we see here an almost unchanged view of the even numbered houses in Vicar Lane.

Six

Beighton Road
to Cliff Wheel

Between the top of Balmoral Road and Station Road, this is still the longest row of shops in the village. Notice how narrow the road is as it enters Market Street.

Looking very elegant, standing by the doorway of Enfield House, No. 4 Beighton Road, are Florence and Lydia Knight. In this 1915 photograph, the two sisters are 'in service' at the residence of Doctor Rae. Shortly after the First World War Doctor Wm O'Brien took over the practice and remained there for around 40 years, until his retirement. Doctor G. Burrows then became the resident GP until he too retired.

From outside the Balmoral Nursing Home we look along Beighton Road. We can see the walls and buildings, on the right, which were later removed for road widening.

Weston House, No. 55 Beighton Road was, for many years, the home of the Hallam family. The main entrance was in the east facing wall but unfortunately the hedge and low wall obscure the two stone lions which were a prominent feature, in the drive, guarding the doorway.

Samuel Charles Blower, born in 1902, outside his home on his pony, *Charlie*. This house, No. 67 Beighton Road, was demolished several years ago, because of mining subsidence.

The Congregational Chapel, built in 1877, and Manse. The last service was held in 1986 after which the building was demolished and the land was cleared. New houses now take its place by the side of the Manse.

The Congregational Community Hall in Greengate Road, behind the chapel, was once used as an Unemployment Centre. This went when the Chapel was pulled down.

Warrens House, as it was known locally, stands high on the skyline in 1950 overlooking that part of the Shirebrook Valley which has now disappeared underneath a refuse tip. Older Woodhouse and Beighton people will remember it as Butlers sweet shop.

Beighton Road, below the Dump-it site, before it was re-routed near the bottom and levelled, to remove the sharp right hand bend. In between the pairs of houses there used to be a lane which led up to six stone cottages. The row of cottages was called Cliff View, but was far better known by its other name, Seldom Seen. The cottages occupied the narrow strip of land farthest from the road.

Here we are looking from Linkey Bank, on the Beighton side of the Shirebrook, across the valley to the four houses seen in the previous picture. This is a 1950s photograph, at this time the row of cottages called Seldom Seen were still standing.

Cliff Wheel takes its name from the site of the water powered grinding wheel, which was a short distance along the path, through a gate on the right. It was built, c. 1805, by George and Thomas Hutton of Mosborough. It was used by them, and by Thomas Staniforth of Hackenthorpe, for the grinding of sickles. In 1879 Thomas Staniforth gave up the tenancy of Cliff Wheel, a decision he had contemplated fifteen years earlier, when one of the sickle grinders was fatally injured by a grindstone breaking. At that time he had complained about the bad state of the machinery. The site of Cliff Wheel is now covered by a landfill site, the road has been straightened and raised and it crosses the link road from the Mosborough parkway to the Aston bypass at a large roundabout.

Seven
Sally Clarks and Birley East Pit

Here we see the well trodden path, from the end of Garden Walk and across the field, to Sally Clark's cottage.

SALLY CLARK'S COTTAGE, WOODHOUSE

The cottage was a notable landmark overlooking the Shirebrook Valley. Originally the roof was thatched. It had variously been known as the White House, Windy House and Gaping Hill Cottage, the latter was its official old name. To those who knew and loved the old village of Woodhouse, with its Picture Palace and winding streets and lanes, Sally Clarks cottage was more than landmark - it was an institution.

The late Mr R.S. Hayman, sub-postmaster of Woodhouse from 1926 to 1952, wrote, 'The four winds of heaven meet at the top of this hill. The air is like champagne and it is said you can sniff the ozone of Blackpool here, Woodhouse people take their air seriously. They claim it is the healthiest place in Sheffield and point to its large number of old age pensioners to verify the claim'. In September 1937 the cottage was scheduled for demolition on sanitary grounds. However, the outcry persuaded the authorities to preserve it, though not for human habitation. However, soon after the last occupants were rehoused the cottage was vandalised. Although Miss Dorothy Birks Ward, Miss Greenwood, Mr Joseph Keeton, Mr J. Hounsfield and others tried to save it, their efforts were to be in vain.

Many of us have memories of kites being flown in the field and of sledging from the crest of the hill. In the summer picnic teas would be enjoyed while listening to the song of a hovering skylark. Children would play there and scores of people would enjoy a walk, perhaps wandering down to the bottom of the hill and over the brook. As we looked back at the cottage, with its whitewashed walls, we knew that just beyond was our village and home.

Howard J. Turner stands by the signal on the Birly branch line, at the bottom of Sally Clarks hill, c. 1950.

VIEW NEAR BIRKLEY PIT WOODHOU E   511

The view south, from Sally Clarks cottage, with the Birley Colliery railway line, linking the east and west pits, in the foreground. The path leads to Rainbow Forge Pond and buildings.

The colliery is shown here from the south west corner. From left to right are the Waddle fan, upcast headgear, three workshops and chimney, the winding house and headgear.

A similar view, showing the spoil heaps taken from the south side of Shirebrook.

The building alongside the chimney is the downcast engine house, in this view from Cannon Lane.

The pit yard in the 1950s. The large building is the washery, to its right is the reserve hopper and, to its rear, the reserve water tower. The No. 1 headgear remains intact with the winding house on the right.

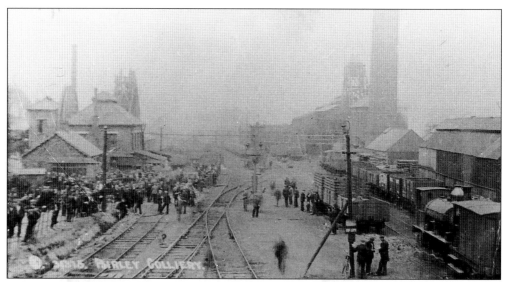

Looking into the pit yard from the footbridge. On the left are offices, the upcast winding house, the upcast headgear and Waddle fan. Across the yard to the right, and from the front is the locomotive *Belsize* and wagons. We can also see the engine shed, the blacksmith's shop, the chimney, the winding house, downcast shaft and screens. The crowd of men gathered around the office were waiting to be paid.

Birley East Colliery First Aid Team 1931. They were the winners of the Sheffield Coal Company Ambulance Shield. From left to right: Ned Brindley (Deputy), Ossie Turner (Instructor), Bill Garder (Captain), Arthur Hutton (Face Worker), Jim Dooley (Manager) and Sid Roberts (Face Worker).

From left to right: George Watson (guard), Jack Ellis (fireman on temporary shunting duties), Ken Atkin (fireman) and Les Ellis (driver). The locomotive is *WDG*, using the initials of William Dunn Gainsford.

Roland Payne is standing below the footplate. Harrison Boulton is in the centre and driver Ted Williamson stands to the right of the cab. The locomotive is *TRG*, using the initials of Thomas Robert Gainsford. Both men were original shareholders of the Sheffield Coal Company, which was founded in 1873.

The Sheffield Coal Company Limited.

EAST BIRLEY COLLIERY.

PARKGATE SEAM.

Machine Face   -   -   Price List.

3RD FEBRUARY, 1938.

THE SHEFFIELD COAL COMPANY LIMITED.
EAST BIRLEY COLLIERY.

PARKGATE SEAM.
MACHINE FACE   -   -   PRICE LIST.

1. To getting and filling machine cut coal, blown as in present practice, as large and as free from dirt as possible, on to conveyors, including the setting of all face props and bars as directed by the Management, with the exception of bars seven feet and over in length which are subject to a separate clause in this Price List. The Colliery Company to bore all shot holes and provide explosives.

   Per ton ... ... 1/- (one shilling)

2. **To dealing with fast ends.**
   To cutting and filling where one fast end exists ... ... 4/6 (four shillings and sixpence) per lineal yard.

   To cutting and filling where two fast ends exist ... ... 7/6 (seven shillings and sixpence) per lineal yard.

3. **Casting back of coal.**
   It is agreed that the tonnage price shall include the casting back of coal to the conveyors up to a distance of ten feet.

   If casting coal over ten feet special arrangements for payment to be made with the Management in accordance with Clause 9.

4. **Dirt falling with coal.**
   In case of dirt or other material above the section normally worked falling with the coal, the following extra scales shall be paid :—

	per ton
Up to 4″ in thickness ...	Nil.
Over 4″ and up to 5″ in thickness	½d. (half penny)
„ 5″ „ „ 6″ „ „	¾d. (three farthings)
„ 6″ „ „ 7″ „ „	1d. (one penny)
„ 7″ „ „ 8″ „ „	1¼d. (penny farthing)
„ 8″ „ „ 9″ „ „	1½d. (three halfpence)
„ 9″ „ „ 10″ „ „	1¾d. (penny three farthings)
„ 10″ „ „ 11″ „ „	2¼d. (twopence farthing)
„ 11″ „ „ 12″ „ „	2¾d. (twopence three farthings)

For the purpose of this clause, measurements to be taken starting at the delivery end and thereafter every 20 yards and the average of these measurements to be the basis for payment under this clause.

The above measurements to be taken on the first day of every week and to determine payment for the ensuing week.

5. **Setting of bars.**
   s. d.
   8 feet wooden bars ... ... 1/- (one shilling)

6. **Allowances for water.**
   per shift
   s. d.
   If wet underfoot ... ... 9 (nine pence)
   Where water rains on men from the roof ... ... 1/6 (one shilling and sixpence)
   No man shall receive both these payments for one shift.

7. **Day rate.**
   Where colliers are working for the Company they shall be paid at the rate of ... ... 7/9 (seven shillings and ninepence) per shift base.

8. **Waiting Time.**
   In the event of any stoppage of over thirty minutes during the ordinary working shift, due to the conveyors, and the men are required to stay in the pit, the men shall be paid for all time over thirty minutes at the rate of ... ... 7/9 (seven shillings and ninepence) per shift base.

   During such waiting period the men must undertake such work they may be called upon to do.

9. Any work done for which a price is not stated in this Price List, the remuneration to be paid shall be arranged between the Management and the workmen concerned, and failing agreement then between the Management and the Workmen's Representatives.

   The above prices are the 1911 basis and subject to general district percentage rates and flat rate payments as per agreement now existing.

Signed on behalf of The Sheffield Coal Co. Ltd.
   T. B ATKINS,
   R. BENNETT,
   E. THOMPSON.

Signed on behalf of the Workmen.
   W. H. MIRFIN,
   A. BRIGGS,
   W. G. GREGG,
   ARTHUR SHAW,
   FRANK HOLMES.

Signed on behalf of the Yorkshire Mineworkers' Association.

   FRANK COLLINDRIDGE.

Eight

Birley Spa

A building in the grounds of Birley Spa, c. 1920.

This building was known as the Bath Hotel when built in 1842 by Earl Manvers. The combined hotel and bath house were built in the Dutch style of architecture which was fashionable at the time and which took advantage of the sloping site. The main doorway is south facing and is approached from Birley Spa Lane. The two floors were connected by an interior staircase with the baths underneath. The terms for bathing are shown on the opposite page. A boiler heated the water for the hot baths. Only the large cold bath remains, it is thought that Earl Manvers removed the marble for use at Thorsby Hall. The baths opened for public bathing on Monday 1 May 1843, George Eadon and his wife had been selected from eleven applicants to manage the place. Their salary was £20 per year with free rent and coal.

Edward Hobson, one of an administrative committee of four men, kept a diary and recorded that on 26 May 1843 'The Duke of Portland from Welbeck came to Birley Spa in his carriage with three horses abreast today. He took a hot bath.' It was recorded that the Duke took further hot baths on the 27 and 28 May 1843. After a stay of over a week the Duke and his retinue left for the Tontine Inn in Sheffield where they had lunch before returning to Welbeck.

In 1845 the charges were reduced to attract more customers, but to no avail. The expenses book showed that the Spa hardly paid its way. Five more managers came and went after George Eadon (who managed the baths until 1848) and by 1895 only one plunge bath remained. The hotel had ceased to function as such by about 1878. The Spa was put up for sale in 1912 and was brought by Mr George Moulsen. The date of the indenture between Moulson and The Earl was 23 April 1913. George Moulsen was a cab proprietor of Woodhouse and he paid £930 for the grounds, building and two cottages. It was he and his partner, Mr Smith, who proceeded to turn Birley Spa into the pleasure ground so well remembered by the older residents of the area.

BIRLEY SPA.

TERMS FOR BATHING.

ANNUAL SUBSCRIBERS.

	£	s.	D.
One Person	0	15	0
Two of the same Family	1	5	0
Three or more of the same Family......	1	15	0

FOR A SINGLE BATH.

Best Marble Hot Bath	0	2	6
Hot Baths	0	1	6
Tepid Bath...........................	0	1	0
Large Cold Bath......................	0	0	6
Ladies Cold Bath.....................	0	0	9
Hot and Cold Shower Bath.............	0	0	9

Annual Subscribers to the Bath Charity of 5s. may recommend One Poor Person; Subscribers of 10s. Three; and Subscribers of 20s. Seven.

☞ *No Bathing Allowed on the Sunday, except by Order from a Medical attendant.*

The bath as seen from the entrance door. It is about 25 feet in length and 5 feet and 8 inches in depth.

A police frogman retrieves debris thrown in by vandals.

A view from the west end of the bath house to the doorway. The interior walls have been improved since this photograph was taken, the bath itself has remained in remarkably good condition since being built in 1842. It was often called the Roman Bath by local people and, long before these baths were built, a man called George Hancock is recorded as paying rent for a building at Birley Spa in 1789. The Roman road, Ryknield Street, passed over Birley Moor from the fort at Templeborough to Chesterfield, the close proximity of the Romans lends credence to the idea of a Roman bath here, but no hard evidence has ever been found to support the claim.

This picture shows the steps into the bath from the west end. The bath had been emptied for restoration work to be carried out.

BIRLEY SPA.

The following is the Analysis of these Springs as made on the Spot,

BY MR. WEST, CHEMIST, LEEDS.

THE LARGE PLUNGING BATH.

Sulphate of Soda .... 7½ Grains per Imperial Gallon.
Chloride of Calcium .. 1   ,,
Carbonate of Lime .. ½   ,,

Total.......... 9 Grains

This is almost pure Water, *such as is now sought after for the Hydropathic method of cure.*

THE CHALYBEATE SPRING.

Sulphate of Soda .... 40 Grains, equal to 75 Grains of crystallized Glauber's Salts.
Sulphate of Lime.... 22½ Grains.
Carbonate of Lime .. ½   ,,
Protoxide of Iron .. 4   ,,

Total .... 67 Grains per Imperial Gallon.

The proportion of Iron in this Water is rather large. The Sulphate of Soda present is a valuable addition, tending to prevent constipation and other injurious effects which Chalybeate Medicines sometimes produce when taken alone. The Carbonic Acid present (11¼ cubic inches per gallon) will increase the tonic powers of the Water, as well as cause it to agree better with the stomach.

TREE. DESTROYED. BY. LIGHTENING
AT. BIRLEY, S P A. JUNE 9th 1907. PHOTO. BY. J. GOOD.

All dressed in their Sunday best, with the exception of the man on the right, these people add interest to the scene. Later a pond was dug in the grounds.

The north facing wall of the building. The balcony was removed in the 1960s due to it being unsafe and the doorway (upstairs, centre) has since been converted back to a window.

One of two wooden dragons, with children of the photographer, Mr Stone, *c.* 1930.

Mr Moulson built a stone retaining wall across the stream of water from the Spa to make the pond. As well as rowing boats and dragons, there was a paddling pool and sands, see saws, swing boats and net fishing for the children. There was a sweet shop at the entrance and walks and bench seats along the wooded hillside made it a delightful place to visit during the 1920s and 1930s, when places offering such entertainment were few and far between.

These two photographs, c. 1930, have, apart from the boats, changed very little. The large tree is still there, as is the path leading down from the bath house.

The

Children's Paradise!

BIRLEY SPA

(Near FRECHEVILLE)

Your Children will simply Revel in the—

PADDLING LAKE (2 feet deep and Curative Water.) SANDS, SWINGS, ROCKING BOATS, SEA-SAWS, NET FISHING, etc. - - -

ALL FREE to Children under 14

OTHER ATTRACTIONS ARE—

Rowing Boats, Motor Boat, The Old Wishing Well

The Famous Zoo Tree, — The Roman Bath —
(noted for its Curative Waters)

Come - and bring the kiddies for the Day !!

TEA AND HOT WATER PROVIDED

Admission to the Grounds — — Adults 2d. — Children 1d.

Swimming in the Roman Bath — — — 6d.

10 minutes walk from Intake Trams. Beighton Buses stop at Spa Lane

SPEND YOUR HOLIDAYS AT BIRLEY SPA !

Manor Press, Printers, Bk. City Road Garage, Sheffield 2.

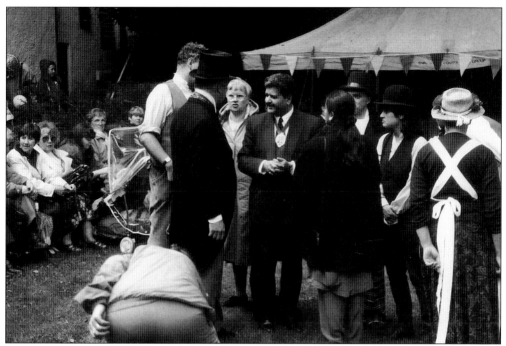

Councillor Qurbon Hussian, the Deputy (and later Lord Mayor), at the opening of the 150th Anniversary Celebration at Birley Spa organised by the Shirebrook Conservation Group and attended by over 1000 people.

The children are appropriately dressed in Victorian costume. The awning in the background was erected for the Woodhouse Prize Band.

A group head back towards the main events after exploring the grounds around the pond. Other events included dancing by girls of the June Fletcher team, steam engines, an electric organ, some machinery, a theatrical group, maypole dancing, tea rooms and displays of information and photographs. The day of 15 May 1993 was a momentous one, celebrating the 150th Anniversary of the only Victorian Bath House with its grounds in South Yorkshire.

Once in danger of demolition, the Birley Spa building, complete with its Victorian Bath, is now a Grade II listed building.

Nine
The West End and Normanton Springs

The cemetery house and chapel were built by William Greenwood in 1878. The cemetery ground was prepared for interments and declared open in the following year. William Haynes was appointed as the first Sexton, here on Stubbin Lane, as Stradbroke Road was then called. The word Stubbin means land covered with tree stumps.

The forty steps leading down to Fairy Dells. Now a distant memory, the valley was filled in, during the late 1940s, before the Stradbroke estate was built. We see here the upper part of the brook which flows through Shirtcliffe Wood.

The grassed area behind the Vestry Hall remains. The Endowed School Room and wall were situated where the road linking Sheffield Road and Chapel Street is now.

Here we see the Endowed School Room and the old Police Station beyond it. Sheffield Road is in the background.

A view from Waterslacks Lane to the old Central Branch of the Woodhouse Coop, in the background. The Endowed school was built c. 1850, then in 1889 the children were transferred to the new school in Station Road, built by the West Riding Authority. Although always known as the Endowed School Room, the building was used as a village hall, for dances and all kinds of social occasions until its demolition, c. 1970.

The house on the left was one of a row of four. Beyond and behind here Waterslacks Lane led to allotment gardens and rejoined Sheffield Road below the Angel.

A soup kitchen during one of the coal miners strikes of the 1920s. Free food was distributed by volunteers to the needy, this included most of the people in the village, judging by the turnout. Behind the two boys standing on the wall is Cowley's pawnbrokers shop.

Waterslacks Lane. The south facing wall of the old Police Station is in the centre of the picture. Le Tall suggests that the lane may have got its name from the kind of coal found there, which had plenty of water in it and was principally slack. It would have been found in the Swallow Wood seam.

This cottage shared the triangular piece of land with the old Police Station.

The lady on the right walks past the entrance into Pashley's cottages and the fish and chip shop. A van driver makes a delivery to Bernard Newbould's grocery shop.

The same place some 20 years later; the shop is for sale, also note the difference in the width of the road.

The gate gave access to the front of No. 46 Sheffield Road, the nearest cottage. The farthest two, in the row of three, were known as Twitchill Cottages, access being gained through the opening on the left. This was known as the Twitchill Path which connects Sheffield Road with Bishop Hill. A modern bungalow now occupies this site.

No. 48 Sheffield Road is the stone built, detached property occupied by the Anderson family. Part of one of the Twitchill Cottages, which have since been demolished, can be seen on the right.

William Widdowson and Charlies Staniforth are seen here on their return from the morning shift at Birley East Pit, *c.* 1907. The clanging sound of clogs and the sight of colliers walking home with coal dust blackening their faces was familiar to all those who lived in mining villages such as Woodhouse. Stanley Widdowson stands waiting for his father, they lived at the house on the extreme right, No. 25 Sheffield Road.

Here we see Helliwells farmhouse and the kitchen which stood directly opposite No. 48 Sheffield Road.

Ken Walton, with his school pal Harold Helliwell, and Lawrence Helliwell in the background. They are seen here in the Helliwells farmyard.

From No. 73 Sheffield Road to No. 81, a shop on the corner (affectionately known as Spark's corner), this property, and all that is seen through the gap on the left, was demolished in 1979. Swallow Wood Court is the new address of the bungalows built on this site.

A new house has been built on the plot of land next door to, and beyond, the house with a canopy. This side of Sheffield Road is otherwise unchanged. The Openshaw family occupied the house and grocery shop. A gas lamp and telegraph pole standing on the left, close to the demolished property, and the houses of Frecheville in the distance, all help to give an approximate date to this wintry scene, of the late 1940s.

The Woodhouse West School was opened in 1900. The picture shows a part of the school being built. The man with the shovel is Mr Young, he stands with another workman in front of a steam driven mixer.

The corner of Victoria Road and Sheffield Road in the early 1930s . In those days it was necessary to have a large pole in the garden to receive satisfactory reception when 2 and 3 valve wireless sets came on to the market.

The two bay-windowed houses and another pair, past the junction of Wolverly Road, were built in 1922 by Mr Rowley, who lived in the nearest one. His business then went bankrupt and the contract was taken over by the City Corporation. The pair of houses on Sheffield Road, nearest to the school, were built without the bays, as were all those in Wolverley Road, Southsea Road and other similar roads. The City Architect occupied the second house during the building period, Mr Rowley was kept on and employed by the corporation.

Families moved into their new homes before the road surface had been laid.

The, almost complete, ladies hairdressing salon at the top of Ashwell Road. This was demolished to widen the top of the road.

Normanton Springs F.C. Back row, from left to right: A. Tame, J. Crossland, A. Froggat, G. Hopkins, -?-, H. Shaw, A. Taylor. Front row, from left to right: D. Rowbotham, -?-, J. Pridmore, J. Wells, -?-.

Normanton Springs F.C., winners of Holbrook Senior Cup and Junior Cup, 1921-22. Top row, from left to right: Mr Briggs, A. Froggat, G. Hopkins, F. Booth, -?-, Mr Bennet, Mr Pidcock. Second row, from left to right: Bob Knight (cobbler), A. Brammer, -?-, J. Pridmore, J. Wells, J. Crossland. Front row, from left to right: -?-, D. Rowbotham, -?-, -?-.

The coronation of King George V and Queen Mary was celebrated at Westminster Abbey on 22 June 1911. This patriotic group made it an occasion to remember in Normanton Springs.

Normanton Springs lost all thirty four of these terraced houses, in 1982, to make way for the roundabout and Mosborough Parkway, which crosses Coisley Hill just to the right of the trees.

The seven cottages of Netherwheel Row were built for the families of the workmen who were employed as sickle grinders at the nearby site.

Several years ago the site of the Netherwheel was excavated. It was one of five sites along the Shirebrook used for the grinding and forging of scythes, sickles and other edge tools. It was built by John Taylor, in 1749, who was granted a lease of land on Woodthorpe Common at the bottom of Coisley Hill. Accompanying the grant was the right to cut and dig out the channels necessary to run water, from the Shirebrook, to and from a wheel. The grinding wheels were hung in the troughs, which were filled with water when in use, to keep the stones wet. This prevented the metal overheating, which would affect the temper of the blade's cutting edge. The grinder sat over and astride the wheel on a wooden 'horsing'.

A particularly bad day, during the severe winter of 1947, stopped this delivery of milk at the top of Normanton Hill.

The school in Normanton Springs was built, in 1871 – 1872, with money left by Thomas Dunn of Richmond Hill House. He was a partner in the Sheffield Coal Company. The two school villas were originally built in the mid-nineteenth century for the manager and under manager of nearby Birley West Colliery.

Ten
Woodhouse People

St James Church Choir. Back row, from left to right: Mrs Heath, Mrs Sharpe, Lilian Anderson, Dorothy Blythe, David Prince, Mr Tong, Mr Prince, Dylis Shaw, Mrs Tebbs, Pauline Morris, George Haigh. Front row, from left to right: ? Fletcher, John Anderson, Glen Gillott, Robert Richmond, Peter Anderson.

Jabez Good, photographer. Towards the end of the last century and well into the present one this man took hundreds of photographs in and around the village of Woodhouse. The cover photographs both on this book and on the 1996 publication are examples of his work. Many of his other pictures have been reproduced on the inside pages. To him we are immensely grateful for providing us with a pictoral insight into the history of Woodhouse.

Walter Goodwin, on his rounds, servicing one of the gas lamps which lit the streets of Woodhouse.

114

The 63rd West Riding Home Guard Unit, based at Birley East Colliery and later at the Wesley Chapel and the Cross Daggers. They formed in 1939 and were disbanded mid 1943. Back row, from left to right: T. Hardwick, -?-, Wilf Walker, Eric Tranter. Forth row, from right to left: -?-, Dennis Mellor, Sam Haywood, ? Morley. Third row, from right to left: Johnny Warington, ? Holmes, Cyril Thorpe. Second row, from left to right: W. Garner, F. Fidler, Ernest Brown, William Lievesley, -?-. Front row, from left to right: Len Keeton, Walter Little, William Hazzard, Lieutenant ?, Alex McQueen, Sid Walker.

A group of Tanyard workers. Oak bark, used in the tanning process, can be seen in the background.

A group of over thirty people visit the Major Oak at Edwinstow, in 1894. Five of the men leave off their headgear for the photograph, but all the ladies keep their hats on.

A proud Mr Scaife (groomsman), with an immaculately turned out horse and carriage, at Holy House. This photograph was possibly taken on the same day as the one below.

William Birks, tanner (1833 – 1895), with his second wife Mary (née Dewhurst). Mr Scaife stands holding the horse.

Birks Bros. AEC Charabanc, at an unknown destination. The ladies seem to have picked a dry day for their outing, but the co-driver is not taking any chances. The cover for inclement weather is rolled back and can be seen behind the rear seats.

In 1925 William Furniss, then aged 61, polled 2,482 votes. His rival was Miss Lilian Atkinson, the daughter of Mr W. Atkinson JP, the President of the Handsworth and Richmond Conservative Association. She gained 1,332 votes, which left a majority for William Furniss, the Labour candidate, of 1,150. Councillor Furniss was the son of a miner, he was a member of the Sheffield Board of Guardians and was President of the Woodhouse District Nursing Association for seven years.

Handsworth Woodhouse District Council Officials visited the houses on Coisley Road in 1919. When built, these houses were leased to the Sheffield Coal Company, when the lease ran out, in 1919, the SCC decided to purchase all thirty two houses. Here they appear to be undergoing major refurbishment. Among the officials are, from left to right: Mr Oates, Mr Powell, -?-, Mr Strong, Mr Rodman (Chairman), Mr E. Atkin (centre) and Mr W. Keeton (next to the end).

The same group of officials at the Stone Lane sewage plant.

Lilac Cottage. The plaque, behind the men forth and fifth from the left, may give a clue to the destination of this outing in 1933.

William Cotterill with the many prizes that he won as a sprinter.

Mr Hare of Church Lane. He had just won first prize at the Woodhouse Show in 1908.

Another soup kitchen group. This one was in Keyworth's Yard, Tannery Street, probably in 1912. Everybody remembered to bring their own jugs.

The last meeting of the Handsworth Woodhouse Urban District Council, in 1922. Back row, from left to right: -?-, Mr Mitchell, -?-, -?-, -?-, -?-, Gus Powell, Ernest Atkin, Mr Powell, Willie Rodman, -?-. Front row, from left to right: -?-, W. Furniss, -?-, Polka Oates, Mr Keeton, -?-.

St Paul's Church Senoir Choir, 3 November 1951. Standing, from left to right: Roy Pendleton, George Ellis, Lilian Ashmore, -?-, Mrs Kirkwood, Freda Phillipson, Audrey Wood, Irene Strong, Greta Bedford, Mrs Warren, Mrs Pendleton, James Kirkwood, Mr Morley, Ena Briggs, Brian Pendleton, Norman Binney, George Bosworth, Phyllis Chapman and Alice Poynton. Other members of the choir include: George Ellis (piano), Clem Pendleton (standing in the centre), Mr Warren (seated).

St Paul's Church Junior Choir, 1951. From left to right: Irene Strong, children including: Norma Wilby, Enid Richardson, Dorothy Phillipson, Hilary Bell, Meryal Hall, and Norma Robinson, then Barbara Strong, Jean Harrison and Muriel White. Also pictured here are: Freda Phillipson (piano) and Victor and Angela Paynton (bottom right).

Woodhouse West School, c. 1931. Back row from left to right: -?-, -?-, Edith Hallsworth, Ken Walton, -?-, Joan Foster, Marjorie Worthy, Harold Helliwell, -?-, -?-, -?-. Forth row, from left to right: Gordon Booker, Doreen Smedley, -?-, Douglas Cross, Fred Lindley, -?-, -?-, Nancy Skeels, Tommy Whitehead, -?-, George Bunker. Third row, from left to right: Minnie Hobbs, Leah Shaw, Doris Williamson, -?-, Ron Porter, Cyril Bramhall, ? Fox, Ernest Morton, Joan Turnbull, Muriel Hare. Second row, from left to right: Jessie Storey, Tony Ward, Stan Clark, Mary Helliwell, Dorothy Wattam, Nora Ward, Ezra Spooner, Colia Hall. Seated, from left to right: -?-, Leonard Widdowson, -?-, Gladys Hare.

VE Day celebrations in Haxby Street, May 1945. Among the ladies are Mona Needham, Mrs Mycock, Mrs Knight, Ada Craig, Herriett Cadman, Nellie Hall, Annie Yeardley, Lissy Needham, Ada Oxspring, Emily Hale, Emma Fuller, Mrs Hall, Mrs Wilby, Mabel Craig, Edith Herbert, Betty Hall, Mary Pidcock and Mrs Gudgeon.

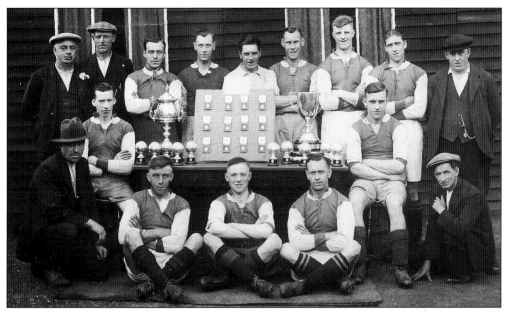

The Woodhouse Working Mens Club Football Team in the 1930s. The group pose outside the wooden hut, which was the clubs first premises. The five non players, clockwise from the man wearing the trilby, are Ernest Morton, N. Hancock, Jack Pridmore, Jobey Cooper and Harry Hall. Many of the team players came from outside the village, so some names are not known. Jack Barrister, wearing a white shirt, stands behind the table.

Doctor Arthur William Scott, MD Brux. 1885, MRCS Eng 1884, LSA 1883, Queens College, Birmingham. This man was the Medical Officer to the Handsworth District of Sheffield Union, certified Factory Surgeon to the Grand Central and Midland Railways and Surgeon to Birley, Orgreave and other collieries. He practised at Woodhouse (and from 1889 was Medical Officer for Health to the Handsworth Urban District Council). He retired in 1924 and moved to Avonhill, 24 Stumperlowe Crescent Road, Fulwood. He had practised in Woodhouse for 43 years and for 30 years had been the Sheffield Coal Company doctor as well as Instructor to the Woodhouse St John Ambulance Brigade. He also carried out infant welfare clinics. (Information supplied by C.H. Shaw, District Community Pyhsician in 1974.)

These Whitsuntide walkers pass the library and The Salvation Army Hall in Tannery Street. The three leading ladies are Ann Newbould, Janet Moore and Majorie Williamson (née Walton).

The 1966 Whitsuntide procession passes A.F Dobson's shop in Cross Street. Two observers watch from an upstairs window.

Unfortunately little is known about this photograph by J. Good of the 1911 - 1912 Woodhouse Amateur FC. Four members of the group on the back row have ribbons in their lapels as if to celebrate a victory, which was perhaps the reason for the team photograph.

A group of Woodhouse Coop employees, in the yard of the old Central Branch, on Sradbroke Road. From left to right: Charles Grundy, George De Bane, Winston Winfield, Luther Holmes (baker) and Mrs Olroyd (cake icer and decorator).

The 173rd (St James) Sheffield Scouts, *c.* 1966. Back row, from left to right: Eric Moody, Raymond Wild, Keith Hayward, Steven LaDell, Steve Harris, Andrew Morris, Donald Kellam, Brian Haley. Third row, from left to right: Mick Joynes, Glen Gillott, -?-, Philip Haley, -?-, Mick Hancock, John Shepherd. Second row, from left to right: Duncan Jeffock, David Fletcher, David Allender, Philip Bray, -?-, -?-, John Sellars. Front row, from left to right: -?-, Paul Bradshaw, Stephen Lockwood, John Williamson, Richard Little, Stephen Moody, Robert Williamson, -?-, -?-.

The St James Mission Church was formed by Captain Murrell CA, in 1927-28. This picture was taken soon afterwards at The World Jamboree held in Arrow Park, Birkenhead in 1929. Back row, from left to right: S. Allison, D. Brunt, C. Jones, L. Banks, W. Brint, J. Robinson. Middle row, from left to right: A. Meredith, H. Platts, O Twynam, F. Morley, A. Niblett. A. Chattaway, H. Gavins, R. Meredith. Front row, from left to right: A. Thorpe, D. Moore, R. Chattaway, A. Tyler.